# THE LONGEST

## FASCINATING FACTS

David Armentrout

e Rourke Press, Inc.
Beach, Florida 32964

PHOTO CREDITS
© Dennis Carmichael: pg. 13; © Don Eastman: Right Cover, pg. 4; © Michele & Tom Grimm/Int'l Stock: pg. 18; © Mike J. Howell/Int'l Stock: pg. 21; © A. L. Katres: pg. 17; ™, ®, & © 1996 Paramount Parks Inc. All Rights Reserved: Left Cover, pg. 10; © James P. Rowan: Title page, pg. 7; © J. Robert Stottlemyer/Int'l Stock: pg. 15; © R. Tesa/Int'l Stock: pg. 12; © Luba Vangelova: pg. 8

**Library of Congress Cataloging-in-Publication Data**

Armentrout, David, 1962–
    The longest / by David Armentrout.
        p.  cm. — (Fascinating facts)
    ISBN 1-57103-129-4
    Summary: Brief presentations of facts about some of the longest things in the world.
    1. Size perception—Juvenile literature. [1. Size.]
I. Title  II. Series: Armentrout, David, 1962-  Fascinating facts.
BF299.S5A765  1996
031.02—dc20                                              96–26509
                                                               CIP
                                                               AC

**Printed in the USA**

# TABLE OF CONTENTS

WALL

The Great Wall of China is the longest wall on earth. The wall was built to keep out invading armies and **nomads** (NO MADZ). Some sections of the wall are over 2,000 years old.

The Great Wall stretches about 1,500 miles, from east to west, in the northern part of China. It can even be seen by astronauts in space.

In 1985, a report from China stated that the Great Wall was once 6,200 miles long!

*Some sections of the Great Wall of China were built over 2,000 years ago*

# SNAKE

The python is among the largest of all snakes. The biggest pythons grow 33 feet long and weigh 300 pounds. They are found in Southeast Asia.

Pythons are **constricting** (kun STRIKT ing) snakes. This means they kill their **prey** (PRAY) by wrapping themselves around their victims and squeezing the life out of them.

Pythons feed on small mammals such as mice and squirrels. Large pythons have been known to swallow small pigs and even goats.

*Pythons can live for more than 20 years in captivity*

## CORAL REEF

The Great Barrier Reef is a chain of coral reefs, islands, and sandbanks. It is the longest reef in the world, as well as the largest structure built by animals. The reef spreads over 1,200 miles in the Coral Sea off the coast of northeastern Australia.

The coral in the reef is made of the skeletons of tiny animals called **polyps** (PAHL ips). The skeletons build up over time, forming beautiful coral. The coral reef provides homes for more than 1,000 kinds of fish.

*The Great Barrier Reef can be seen below the clear blue waters off the coast of Australia*

# ROLLER COASTER

"The Beast," a roller coaster at Paramount's Kings Island in Cincinnati, Ohio, is the longest wooden roller coaster in the world.

As you ride and reach the top of the first hill, your heart races as you see almost a mile and a half of track and tunnels ahead of you.

Amusement parks have always been a big thrill to people of all ages. Roller coasters have been a part of American amusement parks since the 1870's.

*Riders of "The Beast" brace*
*themselves for a thrilling ride*

11

*The Lincoln Tunnel runs under the Hudson River*

*Angel fish are among the many species of fish found swimming in coral reefs*

## MIGRATION

Arctic terns are small seabirds. They **migrate** (MY grayt) the longest distance of any animal. Arctic terns fly from the top of the earth to the bottom every year.

Arctic terns live in icy regions of northern Canada and Alaska during the summer months. Here they nest and raise their young.

Every August the terns fly south to Antarctica, traveling over 100 miles a day. In the spring they return to Arctic coastlines, ending their roundtrip migration of more than 22,000 miles.

*Arctic terns lay their eggs on rocky Arctic shorelines*

RIVER

The Nile is the longest river in the world. It flows north over 4,000 miles through Africa. The Nile begins south of Lake Victoria and ends at the **Mediterranean** (MED eh tuh RAY nee un) Sea.

Many people live along the Nile. The water supply helps people raise cattle and camels, fish for food, and grow crops in the fertile soil along the river.

Hippos, fish, snakes, and turtles live throughout the Nile. The crocodile is probably the most feared creature of the river.

*Many people make their homes along the Nile River*

# WINGSPAN

The albatross, sometimes called a"gooney," is a large **marine** (muh REEN) bird. The wandering albatross is a huge bird with a wingspan as long as 11 feet.

These huge birds use their long wings to their advantage, spending months cruising the oceans.

The albatross even sleeps on the water, returning to land only to breed and nest. When the young hatch, their feathers are brown but turn white as the birds grow older.

*The albatross has the longest wingspan of any bird*

## LONG-DISTANCE AUTO RACE

The Le Mans car race is the most famous long-distance auto race. The first Le Mans race was held in 1923.

The drivers of the high-powered sports cars spend 24 hours speeding on the track just outside the city of Le Mans, France.

Teams of drivers share the time on the track. The winning team and car covers thousands of miles in the 24-hour race. The greatest distance ever covered in the race was 3,315 miles!

*Auto racing is a dangerous yet popular sport worldwide*

Steering & Road Wheels
momo
BUICK
30
momo
Steering & Road Wheels
30
momo
Steering & Road Wheels
BUICK

## TUNNEL

Some road and railroad tunnels cut through mountains. Other tunnels are dug under waterways.

New York City has many tunnels. The Holland and Lincoln road tunnels run over a mile under the Hudson River. The three tubes of the Lincoln Tunnel connect New York City to New Jersey.

The longest tunnel of any kind is a water supply tunnel. It runs 105 miles from the Rondout **Reservoir** (REZ er vwahr), a place where water is stored, into the Hillview Reservoir in New York.

## Glossary

**constricting** (kun STRIKT ing) — drawing tightly together; squeezing

**marine** (muh REEN) — of or relating to the ocean

**Mediterranean** (MED eh tuh RAY nee un) — a sea linked to the Atlantic Ocean and almost completely surrounded by the lands of Europe, Asia, and Africa

**migrate** (MY grayt) — to move from one place to another to nest, raise young, or search for food

**nomads** (NO MADZ) — people who roam from place to place

**polyps** (PAHL ips) — animals with hollow bodies that are closed at one end, such as a coral

**prey** (PRAY) — an animal that is hunted by another animal for food

**reservoir** (REZ er vwahr) — a place where water is collected and kept for use

# INDEX